PRAISE FOR GUT BOTANY
BY PETRA KUPPERS

"*Gut Botany* weaves disability, ecological, somatic, and performance poetry. Throughout, diverse human and more-than-human bodies *touch* with tenderness, violence, joy, and pain. Kuppers tries to be open to 'the all' and how all her senses 'layer and story' so she can write—'palm tingling'—toward healing, sanctuary, and love."

✗ CRAIG SANTOS PEREZ

"In these poems Petra Kuppers slides words into unexpected spaces following rivers of conscious memories and neural networks of unconscious motions. Places become political and politics become visceral. She weaves a way of being in the world with the forces that oppose it and edges of reality and sensation that serve to feed it. Reading these poems we find light, breezes, and resilience."

✗ MARGARET NOODIN, author of *Weweni*
(Wayne State University Press, 2015)

"*Gut Botany* is a capacious assay of corporeal life-support systems. A lingual choreography of interrelation and interdependence forms a generative phenomenology where every point of contact matters. Gendered, sexual, ableist, ecological, and colonial-settler violence is met with fierce and tender resistance. By disarming all forms of tyranny and extractivism, sustainability is possible. This is a work of immense transformative capacity. I am moved by the sheer responsiveness and receptivity that is involved when *blooming out of line as a gender non-conforming nebula*. Find sustenance in this generous resource of movement and change."

✗ BRENDA IIJIMA, author of *Remembering Animals*

"Through a bold new empiricism—attentions drawn to surfaces, new ways to touch and understand touching, and thus new depths of healing—the human/more-than-human relation is rewritten. *Gut Botany* reveals a geospatial philosophy of radical connectedness."

✗ LINDA RUSSO, author of *Participant*

MADE IN MICHIGAN WRITERS SERIES

General Editors

Michael Delp, Interlochen Center for the Arts
M. L. Liebler, Wayne State University

GUT BOTANY

PETRA KUPPERS

Wayne State University Press
DETROIT

Manufactured in the United States of America.
ISBN 978-0-8143-4763-8 (paperback); ISBN 978-0-8143-4764-5 (ebook)

Library of Congress Cataloging Number: 2019954906

Publication of this book was made possible by a generous gift from
The Meijer Foundation. This work is supported in part by an award
from the Michigan Council for Arts and Cultural Affairs.

Wayne State University Press
Leonard N. Simons Building
4809 Woodward Avenue
Detroit, Michigan 48201–1309

Visit us online at wsupress.wayne.edu

Image description: Ancient sturgeon, bony dinosaur scutes, barbels trailing along stony lake floor, charcoal trace. The image repeats throughout the book.

CONTENTS

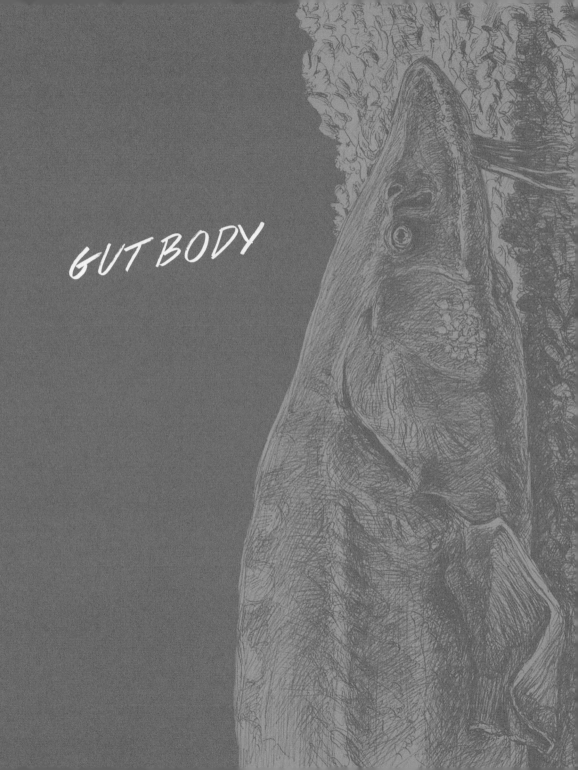

GUT BODY

Sucker punch, the knife in the street
fear of being sheared out of the stream
into the backwater
dead fish belly up by the side of the pond
pills and poisons and endings
let go and sever the ties and ignore
the party is always elsewhere
a shadow in a canoe in a photo
likely put on Facebook tomorrow:
fake of having fun behind
the grass, tree, a Stephen King book
where I know the next sentence already
primacy of white masculine fear
close the leaky gut, body drained of tears.

Just speak, walk with me, close the loop.

Bow forward, pour yourself into your capable hands, and hold your heart.

Bow forward, pour your stomach into your feeble hands, release the binds that bind so tightly to your spinal column.

Bow again, drop your sexual organs into waiting hands, wait. Breathe in, out, in, soothe.

Fish slip into the labyrinth of intestines. Cruise past the atlas, feed
on the carpet fibers of worry.

Agile between the lung pearls, hollow behind the liver, green wall,
delicate black veins spider along for companionship, dark purple,
maroon.

Fins soothe the red spots of tension, white bands where muscles
have leached nourishment out of tight bands.

Between kidney and uterus, raspy tongue licks
soggy dahlias on their stalks, ovaries bloom.

Glide, mucous oils the way. Swim among the velvet.
You, and me, into plump cushions: sturgeon tumbling ground.

Blues

Mark. Into the long lush spiral
curl around a finger's point
your jeans' hesitation
your dark morning tears
the old left side ache
the twisted leg bone
and that tender space beneath your breast
come close to me, come close.
Your criminality becomes legible
in the context of my race. Mark.

I will release you
go and see me drift
far away and loosen
this tight pain
my sadness torn
we stretch
our human fibers wood
tensile, balancing acts
to grow into the
gender-non-conforming nebula.

My blue note soothes you
on the white living edge
of your teeth
I think about the greenness
of bones:
resilient twigs
a bower for me,
our life in the protection of rights.

Safe on the other side
of your mouth
your tongue electric copper
buds open
rising
my blue note soothed
red and blue and red flash
between your teeth
the mouth cave
soft floor.
Mark. "How did these scissors end up in the chest?"
the judge asks her.

I do not live excluded from the certainty
that the legal system exists to protect me,
rhythm runs, undisturbed. Mark.

you.
You.

My hibernation at night
falling time
my pillow and yours
illegible loves
in harmonies
a rest for our blue note
vibration
sensation
red note rising/white.

CONTOURS

This is the inside.
This   outside.
That is your   skin against mine.

Your palm   runs down my front.
Breasts retreat   forward arch
I urge you   on   in   my back.
My toes loop your
                hair. Twist.

You lie across my liver
soften into the heave
       pressed juices
             flow finer   your foot across
thin skin on the inside
my underarm,

my blue vein
open into the green grass.

        Pulse.   Your heel
          callus drags
      t-shirt up trails

bride's bouquet where soft
        white belly blinks.

small beetle finds space
behind your vertebrae
breeze through her old nest
we play, splayed, amid shoots.

Water deep   below. My   shirt

         is damp,

            afterward,

                my face.

You still look poised.

We bear

    on

           the grass carpet.

The beetle wonders
about her short histories.
Birds witness when I burrow
my foot into your armpit.

I kneel,   here,
          ower my face
                    into hollows
feed the pond
          at our feet
          bathe me
                    dark in meadow.

Give way

                                wind

             beetle

                    bird caw.

       Circle overhead

                on your round,

snail-like,

             trace.

COURT THEATRE

I thank the bowl of my hips
I thank the soft edges of my skull
my sternum, big bone presses down
my liver wraps itself around and breathes out toxic
smooth wood and green upholstery
butts butts butts hair and really dark clothes
raised dais at the far end
she calls them to her, conferral, you do not know what is going on
there is code and negotiation
                                        How will you begin?
woman with big silver chains over a lilac patterned blouse gestures
man speaks low, tie straight down and sharp
bewildered clients stare straight ahead
no one looks around
no one looks around

                              Was the performance in line with or a
                              departure from what you experienced?
he pressed down there, and over, the muscles strain
liquid darker this hurts, he does not care and presses, inches
note the finger down and into tender
my breasts mine again now really
spots sore inside bruises
not for any hospital
telephone chains, survivor language, note to speak note
police station marble floor echoes when I make my report
through a window above my head, glassed in, booms

instead suspicion

What happened then?

massage action
I can barely remember now
"are you sure you did not ask for it"

How will you live now?

No. I did not ask
my breast felt, bruised, squeezed hard
fibers spring out of their sockets
shape new contours
body I do not know
I did not ask for that. Why did I not run when I swat away
his hands. Naked. My wheelchair outside. I can't run. I am bound
to these words,
my neck bristles, right now, I write down
these glimpses of memory
words I remember dredging up
for the police woman,
the guy at the station, the man in the suit,

*How did the site influence your
performance?*

The prosecutor in the courthouse.
The corridor.
Outside the bathroom,
consultation, ties, high heels.

*Tell me what you know about
dismemberment.*

No. Tight band across
my breasts, still, never really quite back
into their shape,
the life tenderness, ruptured jelly capsules,
no, I won't go to the hospital, either,
take your hands away now,
take your words away,
your stories of what is
right for massage, and who asks for what,
happy ending jokes,
vulnerable wheelchairs,
the cripple in the waiting room,
who sits on the seats of the court house.
We sit here, legs crossed. She sits. He sits.
We hear stories of robberies.
Is your client pleading

*What was it like for you to see what
you said through another person's body?*

I am pleading to let me out,
let go of my nipples, to stop,
no, I can hardly feel where the hand goes,
around my pubic bone, my leg joint,
femur cracks in its orbit,
there was a hand there, and fingers,
where did the defendant place his hand, exactly,
my senses layer and story

we wheel into the courthouse and I swat away sensation and the
pressure the pressure the blood comes to the surface again, and
prickles in my neck hairs upright, and "this is a classic PTSD
episode," she says, watch the light go and go and go and go and
No. I say, I know I said that, and I repeat it, and you better listen
to me, man tie, "she is the ideal victim," I repeat
what I said just right,

Did your partner's words affect your
body? If so, how?

just exactly, just smooth the way
into the courtroom where we all sit
the lights are on overhead right now
he sits right in front of me,
two rows up, I can see the back of his head,
I do not want to see his face again, ever.
I hold my breasts, my hands cross over.
Skin soft and red, rooted,
breathe into the sternum, deepen, flat,
amulet and a band. Velvet soft green bone.
I thank the fascia snapping back into place.
I thank the blood that is new and red and
can't remember where it went
what it colored. I thank the lungs

Did the performance open up another
way for you to see your own language?

breathe and heave and it's been a year

my kidneys are breathing
it's ok to be thankful and
no, this is not therapy.

What are the consequences of
silence?

this is a fucking

ASYLUM

Rose Cardamom Sea Salt

(upon performing at Earth Matters on Stage, *Reno, Nevada)*

Touch and silk and the rough edges of my fingers catch light
rose lavender bergamot
long hair twists across the plane of the eyebrow and lands, draped,
across a single eyelash
        frankincense
creamy and warmed in the palm it spreads
ocean camel's back sways in the occupied valley
rose cardamom sea salt
sun field crust crystal white rings around blue and green
a red star in your third eye, open
rose lavender bergamot
gather fields, hills, sundrenched and thirsty, a wasp in my hand.
Hay, and a light brown earth, sandy, drains
        frankincense
altar boys, rows deep, red and white. Sneakers peek out beneath
the cassock,
unruly rubble sways through the village, the cross.
Smoke ascends.
Waxen smell grave candles.
Drip red white into the Mars channels of my back, my hand,
pools
where I open a bird.

Now, new seepage, charter wrinkles of a new time,
my hand a ruined
map, not to be rehabilitated, longs
lavender drowsy rose drop
salty taste of my dry desert
        frankincense
forgive all my trespasses
let me enter, in splendor, gracias madre
red and white and purple, under the banner and the monstrance,
my head bows into the depth of your nape.

Asylum

(upon drifting at the Traverse City State Hospital)

Smell of hair, shirt holds
compass of someone's arms, endangered

bed becomes mellow ocean
sails toward an invisible edge

"here be monsters"
racket beyond the door, the Cerberus demands
threshold
nightingale sings at the wrong time,
against the beat again, again.

Too soon, warm gruel

bedpan tilts,

ocean spills into a delta
holds no body

no hyacinth, no round,
no nightflowering jasmine

no wine-dark seas
no camp, no fire

just the dream of sails, away.
The compass of these arms empty

dragons rise when I dream of your eyes
your tongue turns in my heart
the key drops out of my hands
into Jonah's belly, falls,
elevator of despair

knot that won't unfold in the night wind
hurricane
cyclone
howls on the other side of the door
grey corridor with its stripes of green and blue

please please let me
let me
just lie here, pillow swimmer
duvet dreams
blood tick
till the 6pm dinner tray and the yogurt cup
stirred, counter-clockwise maelstrom, for luck.

let me

close the door again and dream of arms

outside

House Concert

*(upon performing at Light Box Artist Space, Detroit, a former Baptist church
and bank)*

What hides under the chairs? What sighs under the upholstery?
Dark forest green moans gothic attic theatres of smooth grey stage
floor, shiny, kick the red brick.

Burnhole into the past snags a tiny hair "Girls Rock: End of
Camp Showcase."

The prophetess sings in the church
hands point skyward,
fingertips in the clouds,
feet in the old vault,
tucked away in a box of earth at night.

The window under the arches is blocked up, no Detroit brick to
sail right through, river right over the whale-sound of authenticity.

There: a shark takes a bite out of the flocked asbestos. Intestine
wires loop inward, rivets high up the wall, pop the screw and my
hips hurt in the decades' damp.

"Today is your day," she sings
her hair weaves into the radiator,
the pavement cracks, amplifier,
microphone, floor cushion,
the empty roll awaits your feet.

German Shepherd mix barks at the *cri de coeur* at the wailing wall at the unicorn hair. Just take it to the bank, just take it to the church, suburban lights mirror ball shoot-out.

The hole in the wall patched up for the camera, for the city inspector decommissions the carpet choir stalls—bricolage living on the liminal riot weed edge.

The prophetess leans into you.
Her skin is warm, her belly peeks
beneath moss-green sweater,
navel opens into another world.

"Everything you feel is appropriate"—the theatre anthropologist in her Sun Ra door blinds sashays across the ceiling tiles scattered by a hurricane.

Ride the inverse ocean, another brick in the sea anemone blossoms on the radiator mesh.

The prophetess is alone on the street corner. Cars drive by. Chain link fence cracks in the winter wind.

Nanook

(listening to Tanya Tagaq in concert with the film Nanook *of the North)*

hollow reed reaches back in time
through the esophagus, through my mouth, vibrates in my throat,
open desert ice air rain, sun blind warm
hollow reed of sea flesh

dark red, pulse, a heartbeat cooled by the arctic water, salt tears
well over my face,
the walrus eyes, the blood rolls down like thunder into the
                    stroke, stroke, stroke
once a kayak faltered, once a river barge, once an ocean liner,
once on Ellis Island, once Ai Weiwei on a Greek beach, once the
boy lay, facedown

mouth buried in the dirty sand, channeled
once men rip into the carcass, strips of fat between yellow teeth,
strap up the buckled knee or die, roll down the throat,
choke and walk,
his mate wallows out in the cold
                    water, water, water

my teeth chew the cow, the pig, the fat of the land and the squeal
echoes only in the tiny bones of our ears, give me your range, in

greed and hunger, give me the peace
in pieces amid climate change, the skin cannot hold oil and water
on the salty faces that go down,
              bow, bow, bow

I chew, rock, swallow, guzzle the oil and the olive trees, dried stiff
on desertified land, the moss inadequate for sustenance, a ration
off the back of a sputtering truck
reedy weeds twine up her legs, sings, stamps, her chest heaves into
touch, open the trough across the sea, the valley of the wave

hollow reed reaches into the migrant chest,
              step, step, step
into the warmth of the liver to process the fat, mercury pearls in
the tissues, silver nitrate ignites

Swing in the Convent

(upon performing in On Higher Ground, *artist Kate Gilmore, Grand Rapids ArtPrize)*

Lift my small wheelchair
over the threshold, you and me:
come home.

Abandoned building gutted
paint red
walls empty, stripped
change ourselves,
shapeshift bosoms tight embrace
cut-off tights. Scapular habit.

Slip into a white dress.
A bride for you,
hung to the right,
no need to look at the x-large labels.

Shoe pair too small,
we hobble with our toes slightly warped
 not far, and up in the air.
Ground-floor left room.
All is painted red.

A huge wooden panel marks
a door that is no longer there.
Parlor, a kneeling stock in the corner,
bible arranged neatly
edges sharply aligned with the grain
and the free wood swings
sturdy black ropes
looped up into the thick
rafters overhead.

Surely they have checked for termites.

I sit on the swing.
Weight lengthens
the ropes half an inch to the floor.

Wooden board sinks into the sockets of my butt,
a familiar rectangle, thighs
squeeze over the red edge.
I start up.
My feet reach straight out,
gentle arc takes them through
just beyond the window sill.
I have to be careful.
Don't lose a shoe here.

I swing.
I listen to the sounds from next door,
another bride swings there,
in the wind,
my bride creaks along.
I can't hear a thing.

Tree rocks, forward and back.
I can't see the pink outside.
My uterus swings in the weeds.
I see red, I see white, I see my darling bride.

MOON
BOTANY

Armchair botany: my
collaborator went on
wheelchair-inaccessible
nature hikes and brought
back found materials for
a creative exchange.

Found on an Oregonian Playa

Barbed wire: do not walk here
if you are a cow, your hooves will puncture and swell
gush bloody puss on the desiccated land
boils explode on the grey cacti, clings on to life,
roots deep in the pores of pumice, treacherous hold,
one gust of the night wind and plants pummel across
the basin, their heads dipped into one shallow bowl
of salty sour water, a mirage, drift past already, gone,
the storm gusts you till you are spiked on farm machinery
and the lever of the long-dry pump of the old corral.
Do not walk here, in the land of light stones and ancient wire,
there is no hold fit for the hitching.

Found in the Cave

Ejected gun shell pops echoes and scars
what might be home for a little club of moles, or
a coyote mama ready to plush her nest against
the pockmarked sandstone wall.
Mice bones: dart between the little lead pellets,
ears twitching against the bat sonar, far below the
long booming plaaaong of the gun which you register
as whisker's gust of wind. With luck, some rain, enough to
moisten the next shelf down, the dry arroyo,
and the kernel that you had left there, with no one
to tell you why, and how a mouse could harvest
the tallness of even a little reddish heirloom maize.

Found on the Pond Deck

The husk of a tiny dragonfly, translucent,
clings upside down on a yellow spear of grass
its roots clasp the dry wood of the deck.
Tiny white fibers everywhere: the planks, breathing,
expectorate their innards, wood weeps and uncoils
what it knew when it stood, tall in a wet Redwood forest,
before the chains of a truckbed, dark and long, bite, here,
where all trees are twisted into themselves against
the prevailing winds. On that white-spun deck,
I remember my watery nature, pour my liquid body
to wash away the pain of the shorter years,
to wash away the pain of a hollow embrace,
the feeling that we all will slide, not into the clear pool,
but into the murk of a place that should not be settled.

Found on the Walk up to the Hill Bench

I might be a horsetail fern, taciturn, very old, indeed,
a bit saggy around the brown bits, the junctures of the segments
that mark my years here in the freezing cold,
in the brutal sun. You call me sparse and elegant,
against the riotous color of the flower carpet all around.
I try to stay alive. You plucked me. Puff ball: do you
have no decorum? Wait to swell, stay around a bit,
let the fibers grow a tad, instead of toddling drunkenly,
waiting to go to seed and spill your guts,
ripe pickings for the thirsty birds or any hand that longs
to squeeze, till innards drip, and watch the world split,
explode, decay, because you can.

Found on the Other Side of the Pond

Inky cap: edible or poisonous, sat out too long in the rain.
Mantle erodes while you look, tears you can use for ink,
these are not black marks, in your book, not the liquids
deliberately mingling with your blood. If your system can't
take transformation, desist, curl your fingers around fluffier
stuff, the cat tail's losing it, too, melts down and pollutes
fine dander with the seedy edge. These lines are not tears.
We deliquesce, bloom out of line, without arthritic shifts,
slipstream on the pond's edge, time alchemies lift
us into multitudes. Your marks edge deeper, compress:
matter out of place accumulates, grooves a canyon,
stiffens your mood.

Found on Mushrooming Walk

Wow, foot print sucker, very flowery chemical
vein not quite in marble.
Old warm sea. Old times. Oh you are so delicate.
You cling on, don't you, beneath the dust of meteorite bowl,
hesitant tentacle preserved and unveiled, immodest,
to the newbies, twinkle mushroom feeds
on air and last night's rain,
pinhead knows nothing of exoskeletal growing pain, rub of dust
on skin chafed by sunburn and the wind's whip.
Stem too delicate to
be picked, a tight little cap peeks for a day at the first hungry bird
without a mushrooming book, extravagant spores ride high
out over the mountain. So, you will live.
Hitch up on boot, dust the sock, lodge yourself,
soar stuck on the windy desert rim, flat stony face.

Found in the Garden

Rhubarb: foreign git from the Volga shores, newcomer,
lushly spreads from the center to lounge and shadow
the soil beneath. No one can understand you. Greenery
will make you vomit. A strawberry cozies up to you,
demure red mantle pricked and juices bleeding to tone
your harsher strings. Now they allow you into pie-shaped land,
tongues smack, entry for your rococo. Then the vole
runs rampant. You continue, crispy mantle unfolds
into the smallest white flowers, do not simmer down,
peek out, arch your back, find delicious roots deep
down to common water source, run elegant, fibers open,
draw, draw, a geyser in the garden, all front, all out.

CRANIOSACRAL RHYTHMS

Craniosacral Rhythms

Earthquakes everywhere my head
hurts till she touches.
Her hand on my forehead.
Her hand on my breastbone.
Blood magma and lymph touch plates
send them shiver,
suspend in skin sacks
the corrugated surface of the cortex.

Fissures and sulci: larger and smaller divisions,
huge surfaces wrapped inward. Our memories fold
around each others' fingers. Let me kiss the spot

where the electrodes fastened to her temples
reset neurons, Frankensteinian fire
old techniques of fluids, electricity, and storms.

Continents beneath, iceberg depth
into the brainstem, reptilian ur-mama flaps her tail,
search for connection. Japan may fold,
California inch further away from Nevada:
we rest here, our plates in thrall with each other,
ping our way into our skulls, cover, cover,
till the borders break open cannot release

member post-traumatic recursions
member vulnerable stories
we burn white bright.

Hot Springs

Crystals invade my bones, my joints,
calm heat pressures raw nerves,
red wounded sites, air chemicals
repair tissue right now.
Feet dangle in the waters sip
thick green. The lining of my mouth
slurps from deep beneath the lake,
salt filtered excretion of a bony land
a homeopathy for my chasmed joints,
rocky cliffs no purchase for soil,
accumulate the blow the wind.
Trees bend.
Do not try to stand up straight.
Indigenous zones.
Rock trail after their erratic journey.
Silica water rushes pearl kernels onto the land,
onto my skin, slips through a hair follicle,
bonds with tired calcium,
frangible and dry, nestles in the splintery
embrace.
Make yourself this place,
bones open into embrace,
my face outward, into the wind's curvature.

Hello

"In 2008 Dennis Jenkins of the University of Oregon reported that
he'd found human coprolites, the precise term for ancient excrement,
dating 14.000 to 15.000 years old in a series of shallow caves
overlooking an ancient lake bed near the town of Paisley." National
Geographic (January 2015)

Someone did pass here, in a band, a mob,
someone who never knew what it meant to be alone,

in vision quest or sanctioned lead of the hunt,
eyes dark and senses open to the burning sun.

Pause for a day and my bones and skin miss
the light touch of the glass fiber, the screen caress, your

affirmation of this—of writing, of a pace
that mirrors yours, my reader—instead

the pond stretches liquid a v-shaped wave
—my headphones etch out birds with k.d. lang—

the cricket remembers the taste of the copper wire, current
murmurs along the highway behind my cabin

shift my fingertips on the keys, into her body
on the horizon line, meet the baton

in the electronic print, revolt, and here it stops.

Someone did pass here, walked the land into their bones,
each generation passing on their way from coastal harvest, without

longshoremen and harbor fire, to ochre caves or a lush inland sea.
An ancient alligator burrows into the mud and expires.

Stop of wire wifi the netted frame of day.
Rest here, do not press the reload button—and still

alone. Rest one night in a small cave, an overhang, barely
protect you from the rays, morning shit bonded with calcite, dried,

salt eats into ancient seeds, skin gently cracked by digestive juice.
DNA wove itself into a message rhythm, amino acids

clouding one by one amid rain and acid and rain and snow
sunbaked pearl lifts itself to the light.

What becomes of the writers' cottage on the dry lake rim?
Whose bodies shapeshift protest in nuclear futures?

My keyboard sips the juice, the black snake in the sky hums
and waits, slips into the wrinkle before the generator

thrums once again, a downward stroke,
someone beats utopia out of my sister's skull.

Alone, we stitch the line as best we can, our hands raised up to the sun, my feet on the salty lines of the alkaline desert.

Hello, she said, 15.000 years later, hello
my Mars Rover, my metal plate, an Eve extends her hand

as if I could decode, in writing, the prayer on her lips,
a call for the bird, for the bison,

for the skin that would guide her
to the other world, of the message freed

circling amid the outer stars
meteor shot back to the forest

of urban strife, the policeman's bullet
from the future desert, hold her saliva drop,

eyelash, smear from the growing cells
of her cervix. Here you rest,

sweet one, thunderbird booms
across the horizon, metal pierces

sunspot's radiant warmth.

Remember the Dinosaurs

Clear path to the lake.
I lay out the Nemo blanket.
Six-year-old cheddar.
My water bottle.
Remember orcas.
Pad Thai, one last time.
Now I sit, knees drawn up
to the chin, water cool.

Old hoot on thin legs
swivels red eyeliner
level with the tree whips.
Whoops chase the intruder
into the blue. I swim, orange floatie
hydroplanes back to the beach.
On the wave, I follow
sky path of feathers.
Cicadas hum.
Remember the gazelles.

Wagner, favorite cat, diabetes dead
crawled deep under the eaves.
Mress cat, a car got him not long after,
swoop over the street,
I hope he was in flight.

Aircraft rumbles invisible
contrails with mosquito whine.
Downshift. Stumble in the still
air. Blue meets at speed with
Pterodactyl hide, errant wings
wrap sun-dried leather
around ceramic blades.
The turbine coughs.
Sound arcs out of the sky.

Meteorstrike, beyond the woods,
new neighbor lake
echoes in the undertones.
Earth displaces cloud geyser
up to the supermoon.
I drip algae, then go home.
Remember your skin.

At night, the cranes rock in the reeds, frogs vibe with the tide,
earthworms attracted by fresh soil and promised rain weave
a living carpet over the metal bubble. A hiss of cooling lapis lazuli,
amalgam of lava-hot veins pipe brittle
before the water booms in.

Endocrine System

Missile system guides rockets in from far away
squirrel doesn't know why
it jumps from leaf-mount up
heart goes heavy at abandoned document
pancreas spreads to keep the heat
chirps upward right into

joysticks at side of my neck funnel into
two devil's horns, snail's eyes, stalks away
for where the river brings heat.
Wider web transmits silently why
energies connect this tree document
and that, dark orange leaves may bounce up

off darker pylons, over, over, and up
what the snail saw and what tries desperate into
connection, pings in, hones on signal document
heartbeat, heat trace, hormonal whiffs away
over mulch and mud ask why
hands hold my thyroid, palm lines heat

to spread their longing heat,
faint tremor, pulse rapidly up.
Can they hear, the organs, shriveled, why

can they sense and touch into
these webs of tender, turn away
river water and blood document?

When does the bark harden into document,
winter comes and kills heat?
One last time beetle tries to get away,
handbag's suede scale up and up.
Squirrel eats the acorns that shimmer into
why, goose does not know why.

Fly paths are called for this reason, why
fixed plans, when to document
inner compass of new futures into
flesh blossom, trust river's new heat,
in the turtle's shell, heron looks up
it is dinner time far away.

Wind Tongue

I go blue, I drop out I go and I skirt school and work and I run
away and I go
forest I won't I won't I shall not and I leave now and here I am
red cardinal pecks in the dirt far behind
water rushes past sleeping snakes
babe dragons with rattles that shake in the wind when they dry,
summer dreams deep beneath ice cold water
vernal peepers North Face hikers
Canadian geese step into sweetly mown grass path
verging along the river drops into black mud
stiff on my cowboy boots I tumble
tree   wind   shake
elasticity of the young snakeskin bark
tissue high and erect as I stroke into a fit between
softness of my palm and crocodile that rears along the way
bits branch out and skewer
eye poke ear pierce
stumble and relax
when   I give my weight   when I give in
when I bow into you and past spears
you echo, sway, far off cars meander through net
muscle flexed   cambium shaken   wind storm
memory
a scream near the nature center

kids spurt tremble earth and bridge and mud on the path
where I try to try to try again to try to reach to my childhood,
play, to lean, to be
all natural, open, to be open to be to be to live to breathe and to
be and to cycle through land and forest is open is open is alive is
try is bridge is memory spur is a spear is an eye and a socket and a
yell and a muscle and a bow a bow a weight a tremble a sleep and
a dark dark wind and a bridge and a dark and now it's too much
and it hurts and I feel all the pinch all pressure all the all the all
the all the leave it and let it and drop this and why.
So I sit down and write, palm tingling with the bark's rough
tongue.

Red dragonfly segmented
shelves of torso, pelvis fly
—phyla structures a discursive
regime I name ancestral knowledge.

Wild Rice Moon

I cannot look you in the eye.
Segmented multitudes, reflect
no ego spreads through antennae
sensitive bristle foot pad hair.

Leaves Changing Color Moon

Skin I, hair I, plates
turn against one another
white glutinous pivot.
Where do you touch me?

Leaves Falling Moon

We meet, moments, hairs out,
align along my pelt.
Then we part. Velcro hairs tug
hooks under my skin, raise a bruise.

Freezing Over Moon

We lift off from one another, molecules
twinned, a touch archeology decoded
by pathologists, were we to die, here
splayed yards from one another by the lake.

Little Spirit Moon

I am not spared precarity
in my occupation of indigenous lands.
I cannot see the lake the way you root
drum, burn the chitin, an alarm.

Big Spirit Moon

We live, you and I, hooks and all
our touch plates out, hum
armor invitation, a heartbeat
lean in, tonight, the Sturgeon Satellite

Sucker Fish Moon

sleep weaves melatonin waves
red blood, white blood, pulse, pulse
older insects hum a thousand
dark eyes in our dream.

Crust on the Snow Moon

POET
DRAG
KINGS

Go to the Brown's, buy a Felinfoel and ask for me, they know where
I live...
Visiting Dylan Thomas's pub in Laugharne

Dylan, you were the life of the party,
thirtynine dead in the Chelsea Hotel.
You beat your wife
that's mainly what I remember.
Some lines of some poems.
Richard Burton's voice.
We listen deeper
un-know colonial   living on   old-rock land.

I have survived you.
So has the woman I love,
most people I know.
Life in the forties. You missed out

on laughter lines, the longer duration.

        Drama ebbs   wider pools.

I stand next to myself
watch
my chemical emotions,

enough   time to tick
seconds between my tears
and me. On these cobblestones,
did you count
nights
you woke with your mouth fuzzy,
brain beat with sluice of blood?

The rivers of the night piss beer in the back alley.

Dylan, we are here. Sip our waters on your unpaid tab.

Liver deltas out
coal towns and ovens,
dampness of spirit
sparks in the summer sun.

We have survived you.
Our hips angled and cushioned,
small automatic car,
wrinkles feathered
into future.
Our lines peel
our fingertips.

Every day, I wake up.
My jagged hip stems
stretch to the side,
the cat who longs to get wet,
who wants to run
along river's edge, ocean pound,
the green fuse drives the flower.

My hotel bed fingers trail her edges,
odalisque in half-light,
sleeping dignity
calmness and quest.
She stretches, I mount,
spoon, listen, she smiles.

We part the waters.

FIELD NOTES

Gut Botany charts my body/language living on indigenous land as a white settler and traveler. My writing grounds itself in surrealist and situationist techniques of dérive and freewriting: losing myself in land, letting my attention drift as I wheel myself through space, notice how the land heaves, the lines of my wheelchair's glide, how strata of occupation shape urban and rural scenes. Some of the writing emerged after engaging with Andrea Olsen's *Body and Earth* curriculum, an environmentalist/experiential anatomy text.

The collection owes much to my friendship with Margaret Noodin, an Anishinaabemowin poet and linguist. She, Jasmine Pawlicki, and the other women of the Miskwaasining Nagamojig/Swamp Singers taught me much about the land where I live now, Michigan, stewarded by Niswi Ishkodewan Anishinaabeg, the Three Fires Confederacy: the Ojibwe, Odawa, and Potawatomi.

COURT THEATRE

Healing from sexual assault by a body-worker is central to *Gut Botany's* journey. I remediate lines from disabled dance artist Perel's performance experiments and Bhanu Kapil's interviews from *The Vertical Interrogation of Strangers* (2001). These seeds point outside of the cage of my memories to the frameworks of performance as wayfarer, embedment, community.

ASYLUM

This sequence emerged out of the Asylum Project performance experiments, co-directed with dancer/poet Stephanie Heit. Our Asylum inquiry explores multiple meanings of "asylum": from asylum seekers and the limits of Empire, to psychiatric asylums and queer sanctuary space, to temporary places of security and refuge. Woven into the poems appear leanings from Taylor Mac and other performance artists.

MOON BOTANY

This series began as an exercise in armchair botany: visual artist Sharon Siskin went on wheelchair-inaccessible nature hikes and brought back found materials for a creative exchange. She arranged the physical objects on the wooden table of our artist-residency hut in the Oregonian outback, and I provided new narratives and containers.

POET DRAG KINGS

This sequence is set in Wales, more specifically, Dylan Thomas's favorite pub (and some of his lines find their way into this drift).

ACKNOWLEDGMENTS

Three parts of "Moon Botany" have been published in *About Place*, two others in *Wordgathering*, some (with a craft essay) in a folio for *Aeolian Harp*, and others (with a writing prompt) as part of *In Corpore Sano*.

Shorter versions of "Gut Body" and "Court Theatre" are in *Imaginary Theatres*, and the full version of "I Thank the Bowl of My Hips" appeared in *Wordgathering*.

A version of "Blues" appeared in *Adrienne*.

"Rose Cardamom Sea Salt" appeared as "Even Song" in *RFG*.

Four sections of "Bug Junction" appeared in *Barzakh*.

Different versions of "Bug Junction," "Contours," and "Hot Springs" appeared in the *Precipice Collective Anthology*.

"Asylum," "Swing in the Convent," and "Craniosacral Rhythms" appeared in *White Stag*.

"House Concert" appeared in *Bombay Gin*.

"Hello" appeared in *Nomadic Journal*.

"Endocrine System" appeared in *Bone Bouquet*.

"Poet Drag Kings" and "Wind Tongue" appeared in *cream city review*.

"House Concert" appeared as part of "Invited Hauntings in Site-Specific Performance and Poetry: The Asylum Project," *RIDE: Journal for Applied Theatre and Performance* 23, no. 3 (2018): 438–53.

"Asylum" also appears as part of "Blood Compost: The Asylum Project," *P-Queue* 15 (2018): 47–58.

✗

My first thanks go to the lakes and waters that held and embraced me. I traveled from the animate, inhabited, and polluted rivers, streams, and lakes of my native Germany to the differently animate, inhabited, and polluted bodies of water in Michigan, and I thank all who work to restore and keep our rivers, lakes, and oceans in balance.

My thanks to the Nibi Water Walkers, whose ritual work influenced the performance actions that led to these writings, and to the elders and leaders of the Idle No More movement, who all remind us that water is sacred. "As we heal the water we heal all of life."

I also want to thank the sturgeon revival undertakings in Michigan, including the spawning reefs in the Detroit River. I am grateful in particular for the hospitality of the Lake Superior State University Aquaculture Lab in Sault Ste. Marie. Knowing that these ancient survivors cruise below the waters has been a powerful guide for my own journey and transformation.

I want to point to activism around vanishing and killed Indigenous women in our border region, including the National Indigenous Women's Resource Center and the Native Justice Coalition's MMIWG2S Project. Organizations like these highlight the terrible effects of racism, settler colonialism, misogyny, and the flawed laws and procedures around domestic violence, sexual assault, and tribal/federal legislation.

My thanks also go to the Ann Arbor SafeHouse Legal Advocate who offered her assistance in the preparation of my trial and to the police woman who investigated my case, but not to the police men who made me speak out loud in a public space what happened to me. I don't want to go further into the personnel and procedures of the legal aspects of my assault, but many people were helpful and supportive, and many were not. Ultimately, I won a conviction, at a price to myself, and I want to mark that this resolution is out of reach for so many assaulted people.

Social media was a large part of my recovery system at the time: sharing and being witnessed at a distance. I am thankful for the support around my court dates, in particular. At one point, I sailed into the courtroom on a wave of Women and Gender Studies professors, all from different universities and colleges in Michigan. That image was very sustaining.

I thank my friend Beth Currans for sitting with me throughout.

I thank my teachers Margaret Noodin, Jasmine Pawlicki, Marsha Traxler Reeves, Stacie Sheldon, Karen Schaumann-Beltran, and the other women of the Miiskwaasinii'ing Nagamojig, the Swamp Singers, a women's hand drum group grounded in language revitalization, and the two language elders who let me be part of two semesters of Anishinaabemowin language instruction, Alphonse Pitawanakwat and Howard Kimewon.

My thanks to the artist residencies that allowed me to shape my Michigan writing: Playa, on an Oregonian salt lake, the Hambidge Center in the Blue Ridge mountains, who took us in when Hurricane Matthew displaced us; the Thicket, on a Georgia barrier island; Surel's Place alongside the rushing Boise River in Idaho; and Vandaler Forening in Oslo, amid the beautiful fjords.

I want to thank big beautiful Lake Michigan herself, my small (shall remain anonymous) local spring-fed lake and its active queer culture, and the Huron River, plus all the insects that still buzz around, even in the midst of international species collapse.

As always, I thank my art/life community, the Olimpias disability culture collaborators and my co-dreamers in Turtle Disco, the somatic writing space I co-create with Stephanie Heit in Ypsilanti, Michigan, my home.

Warmest thanks to my reader, comrade, and friend Denise Leto, and to visual artist and dear co-dweller Sharon Siskin. Thanks to the readers who commented on poems in process: Perel, Beth Currans, Sophia Galifianakis, Amber DiPietra, Daphne Stanford, and my anonymous peer-readers.

Thanks to the Black Earth Institute, dedicated to re-forging the links between art and spirit, earth and society; and my wonderful fellows in the 2018–21 cohort. Thanks to my EcoSomatics workgroup at the University of Michigan, and to all our guest speakers, facilitators, and playful beings.

Thanks to Annie Martin and the team at Wayne State University Press for their enthusiastic support and care.

Most of all, deepest gratitude and honor to my wife and creative partner, Stephanie Heit, a poet and dancer who offers collaboration, nourishment, and joy in her art and life practice.

ABOUT THE AUTHOR

Petra Kuppers is a disability culture activist, a community performance artist, and a professor of English and women's studies at the University of Michigan. She is author of the poetry collection *PearlStitch*, the queer/crip speculative story collection *Ice Bar*, and multiple academic books. She lives in Ypsilanti, Michigan, where she co-creates Turtle Disco, a community arts space.